WAR MACHINES   **SELF-PROPELLED HOWITZERS**

The M109A6
Paladins

by Michael and Gladys Green

Capstone
press
Mankato, Minnesota

Edge Books are published by Capstone Press
151 Good Counsel Drive, P.O. Box 669, Mankato, Minnesota 56002
www.capstonepress.com

Library of Congress Cataloging-in-Publication Data
Green, Michael, 1952–
    Self-propelled howitzers: the M109A6 Paladins / by Michael and Gladys Green.
    p. cm.—(Edge books. War machines)
    Includes bibliographical references and index.
    ISBN 0-7368-2723-4 (hardcover)
    1. M109 Paladin (Howitzer)—Juvenile literature. I. Green, Gladys, 1954–
II. Title. III. Series.
UF652.G74 2005
623.4'2—dc22   2004002004

Summary: Describes the M109A6 Paladin, including its history, equipment, weapons, tactics, and future with the U.S. Army.

Editorial Credits
Katy Kudela, editor; Jason Knudson, series designer; Molly Nei, book designer;
    Jenny Bergstrom, illustrator; Jo Miller, photo researcher; Eric Kudalis, product
    planning editor

Photo Credits
Corbis/Reuters NewMedia Inc., 29
DVIC, 6; Anita Johnson, cover, 23; Don Teft, DAC, 11; PFC Michelle Labriel, 12;
    SPC Jessie Gray, 15, 20
Getty Images Inc./Chung Sung-Jun, 27; Scott Nelson, 21
Michael Green, 9, 19, 24–25
United Defense, L.P., 5, 16–17

Edge Books thanks Scott Gourley for his help in preparing this book.

1 2 3 4 5 6 09 08 07 06 05 04

Table of Contents

CHAPTER 1

The M109A6 in Action

A unit of U.S. Army tanks is on patrol in an enemy country. The tank unit comes under fire. The enemy fires antitank missiles. These missiles could destroy the U.S. tanks. The U.S. tanks stop and move back. The tank commander calls for support.

A group of M109A6 Paladins is 3 miles (5 kilometers) behind the tank unit. U.S. Army soldiers quickly prepare six M109A6 Paladins for a mission. A soldier types the enemy's position into a computer. The computer finds the firing data for the Paladins' cannons. The Paladins fire their cannons. In less than two minutes, the enemy forces are destroyed in a series of explosions.

M109A6 Paladins fight in groups.

LEARN ABOUT:

M109A6s in battle

History of the M109A6

M109A6 design

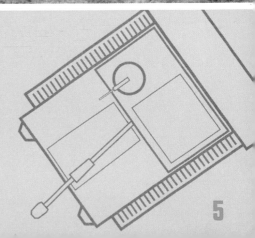

The Paladins move to a new location and fire antitank mines. When a round reaches the area directly over its target, it explodes. The antitank mines fall to the ground. The threat of exploding mines keeps the enemy tanks from moving forward.

The M109A6 provides support from behind the front lines.

An enemy pilot flying a plane over the battlefield sees the Paladins. The pilot drops bombs that explode near the vehicles. The Paladins are armored. No damage is done.

Minutes later, an enemy rocket lands near the Paladins. It releases a cloud of poisonous gas. The gas does not bother the Paladin crews. Each vehicle is equipped with an air system that keeps the air inside clean.

The enemy forces soon find the Paladins are equipped with more powerful weapons. The enemy forces retreat. The Paladins are quickly reloaded with ammunition. The crews get ready for the next battle.

M109A6 Paladins

One of the first modern self-propelled howitzers was the M109. It entered service in the U.S. Army in 1963. The Army continued to improve its M109 series. The Army updated and built new models of the Paladin. In 1992, the Army put the M109A6 into service. The Army currently has 950 of these Paladins.

Self-propelled howitzers are different from other weapons. Many other weapons are towed. Towed weapons have wheels like a trailer. They need a large vehicle to move them. A self-propelled howitzer is mounted on its own vehicle.

The M109A6 Paladin looks like a tank. It runs on tracks and has an armored cab. The M109A6 has a built-in 155 mm howitzer cannon. This cannon is called the M284.

The M109A6's battlefield role is to support the Army's tanks. The Paladin also supports other combat units.

The M109A6 has been in service since 1992.

CHAPTER 2

Inside the M109A6

The main section of the M109A6 Paladin is the armored hull. The hull's armor protects the vehicle from enemy weapons. The hull supports the suspension system the vehicle rides on. It also supports the vehicle's rotating armored cab. This cab holds the Paladin's cannon.

Engine

The Paladin is powered by a diesel engine. The engine gives the vehicle a top speed of 38 miles (61 kilometers) per hour.

LEARN ABOUT:

Hull

Tracks

Crew

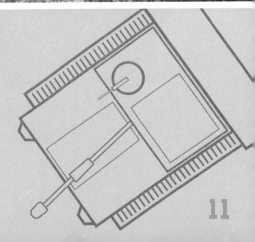

Suspension System

The Paladin's suspension system has 14 wheels on two tracks. A track is located on either side of the hull.

The Paladin also has shock absorbers on the front and back of the suspension system. Shock absorbers help cushion bumps as the Paladin moves across rough ground.

Crew members repair the worn tracks on a Paladin.

Vehicle Safety

The U.S. Army designed the M109A6 Paladin with safety features. The hull and cab of the Paladin are made of armored plates. These plates help protect the vehicle and crew in combat. The Paladin also has spall liners inside the cab. Spall liners are made from the same material used in bulletproof vests. These liners stop metal pieces before they can enter the inside of the vehicle.

Fire has always been a threat to ground vehicle crews. Enemy weapons that break through the hull can start fires inside. The Paladin has an advanced fire suppression system. If sensors detect a fire, the system puts out the fire before the crew can be harmed.

Crew Positions

The Paladin has four crew members. The crew includes a driver, a vehicle commander, a gunner, and an assistant gunner. The crew members talk to each other through an intercom system. Headphones and microphones are built into the crew members' helmets. The vehicle commander can use a radio to talk with people outside the vehicle.

The driver sits in the vehicle's front section. The driver can look through three vision blocks. At night, the driver can replace one of the vision blocks with a night vision device.

The vehicle commander sits in a small compartment called a cupola. It can rotate all the way around. The vehicle commander looks through a set of vision blocks. These vision blocks allow the commander to see all around the vehicle.

The gunner sits to the left of the cupola. A telescope is in front of the gunner's seat. This telescope helps the gunner aim at targets.

The assistant gunner loads ammunition. The Paladin's ammunition is kept on racks. The assistant gunner places the ammunition into a ramming device. This device loads ammunition into the cannon.

Crew members wear helmets equipped with headphones and microphones.

The M109A6 Paladin

Function:	Self-propelled cannon system
Manufacturer:	United Defense, LP
Date First Deployed:	1992
Length:	32 feet (10 meters)
Height:	12 feet (4 meters)
Width:	10 feet (3 meters)
Weight (fully loaded):	29 tons (26 metric tons)
Engine:	440 horsepower diesel
Firing Range:	19 miles (31 kilometers)
Top Road Speed:	38 miles (61 kilometers) per hour
Fuel Capacity:	133 gallons (503 liters)
Crew:	4

1 Armored hull

2 M2 machine gun

3 M284 cannon

4 Tracks

5 Wheels

6 Armored cab

3

Weapons and Tactics

The M109A6 Paladin is equipped with a powerful 155 mm howitzer cannon. The M284 cannon is mounted on the vehicle's cab. The Paladin also has a machine gun on the cab.

M284 Cannon

The M284 cannon can be raised almost straight up. When the barrel is pointing up, rounds can reach targets behind hills and buildings. The M284 cannon has a range of up to 19 miles (31 kilometers). It fires up to four rounds per minute.

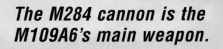

LEARN ABOUT:

Howitzer cannon

M2 machine gun

Paladin platoons

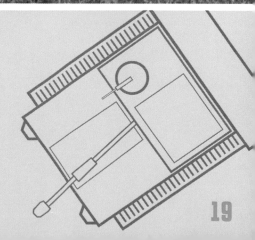

19

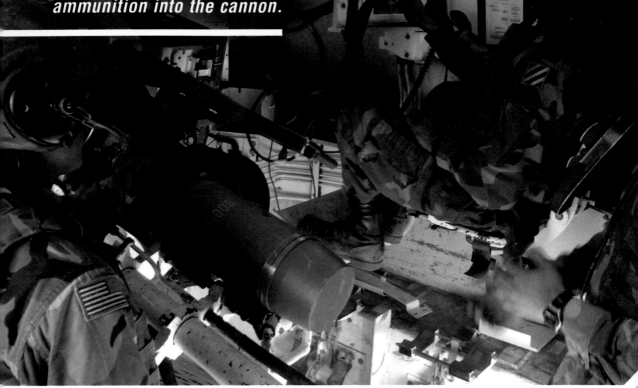

The M284 cannon can fire different kinds of ammunition, including high explosive (HE) rounds. HE rounds are deadly to unarmored vehicles. The cannon can also fire rounds that carry small antitank mines.

The M284 cannon can also fire smoke rounds. Smoke rounds do not destroy a target. When they explode, they release thick smoke. The smoke hides the movement of U.S. soldiers on the battlefield.

The M284 cannon fires different kinds of ammunition.

Machine Gun

The M2 machine gun is mounted on the front of the vehicle commander's cupola. The M2 can shoot 550 rounds per minute. It has a range of 1.2 miles (1.9 kilometers). The M2 machine gun can also fire single shots.

The M2 earned fame during World War II (1939–1945). The Army discovered the weapon could destroy several types of targets. These targets included enemy ground vehicles and low-flying aircraft.

Long-Range Support

The main job of the M109A6 Paladin is to provide long-range fire support to U.S. Army tanks and soldiers. The M109A6's cannon is able to destroy distant enemy targets.

The M2 machine gun can destroy enemy ground vehicles.

Paladins fight in groups. The smallest unit is a platoon. A platoon includes three M109A6 Paladins. A Paladin platoon also has three M992A2 Field Artillery Ammunition Support Vehicles (FAASVs). These vehicles are armed with a machine gun. Each FAASV carries 93 extra rounds of ammunition for the Paladin.

A support vehicle carries extra ammunition for the M109A6.

The M109A6 Paladin's large size makes it an easy target for enemies. Paladin crews try to stay far away from enemy tanks. Paladins fight in groups, but they do not travel together. Each individual unit travels by itself. This system of travel helps lower the chances of being an enemy target.

CHAPTER 4

The Future

The M109A6 Paladin is an important Army weapon. It can destroy targets from miles away. This self-propelled cannon system provides help to Army tanks and soldiers in battle.

Crusader

Before the last Paladin was built, the U.S. Army had plans for a new vehicle system. The Army named the vehicle system the Crusader Advanced Field Artillery System. It featured two vehicles that worked together. These vehicles were a self-propelled 155 mm howitzer vehicle and an ammunition resupply vehicle. The Crusader was scheduled for service in 2008.

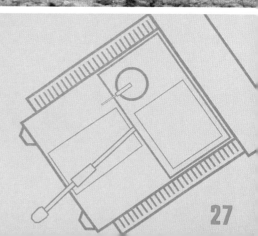

The M109A6 helps protect Army tanks and soldiers.

LEARN ABOUT:

Crusader program

Smart rounds

New weapons

In 2002, the secretary of defense canceled the Crusader program. Only two models of the Crusader vehicles were built. The reasons for ending the program included its high cost, heavy weight, and large size. But the Army will use the information learned from this program for other projects.

Weapon Upgrades

The Army is currently developing long-range smart artillery rounds for the Paladin. Smart rounds can find and hit targets on their own. The gunner does not need to aim the weapon perfectly.

One of the Army's newest weapons will be the M982 Excalibur Extended Range Guided Projectile. The Excalibur is equipped with a Global Positioning System (GPS). The GPS has a satellite receiver. Satellite signals tell the Excalibur how close it is to a target. If the target moves or a better target is found, the Excalibur can change its flight path.

The Excalibur uses different kinds of warheads. The high explosive warhead is used against enemy shelters. An antitank warhead is used against enemy tanks. This warhead holds 64 small bombs that shower down on a target area. Each small bomb has miniature radar that searches for a tank. After a bomb identifies a tank, the bomb guides itself to the tank and destroys it.

The Army's new weapons will increase the usefulness of the M109A6 Paladin. The Paladin has become an important weapon against enemy forces. It will be a part of the Army's future.

The Army's future plans will include the continued use of the M109A6.

Glossary

ammunition (am-yuh-NISH-uhn)—rounds, missiles, and other objects that can be fired from weapons

armor (AR-mur)—a protective metal covering

cab (KAB)—a rotating structure on top of a howitzer that contains a cannon

cupola (KUHP-oh-la)—a one-person armored cab mounted on a larger cab

howitzer (HOU-uht-sur)—a cannon that shoots explosive shells long distances

hull (HULL)—the outside structure of a military vehicle that supports the other vehicle parts

platoon (pluh-TOON)—a small group of tanks or vehicles that work together

range (RAYNJ)—the maximum distance ammunition can travel to reach its target or the distance that a vehicle can travel without refueling

round (ROUND)—a single shell fired by a gun

track (TRAK)—a strip of steel covered with rubber padding; a track runs over the wheels of a Paladin.

warhead (WOR-hed)—the explosive part of ammunition

Read More

Bartlett, Richard. *United States Army.* U.S. Armed Forces. Chicago: Heinemann, 2003.

Cooper, Jason. *U.S. Army.* Fighting Forces. Vero Beach, Fla.: Rourke, 2004.

Sievert, Terri. *U.S. Army at War.* On the Front Lines. Mankato, Minn.: Capstone Press, 2002.

Internet Sites

FactHound offers a safe, fun way to find Internet sites related to this book. All of the sites on FactHound have been researched by our staff.

Here's how:

1. Visit *www.facthound.com*
2. Type in this special code **0736827234** for age-appropriate sites. Or enter a search word related to this book for a more general search.
3. Click on the **Fetch It** button.

FactHound will fetch the best sites for you!

Index